The Collected Poems of Elma Stuckey

For Robert Zangrando —

With continuing Respect,

Sterling

4 April 2000

The Collected Poems of Elma Stuckey

Introduction by E.D. Hirsch, Jr.

Precedent Publishing, Inc.
Chicago   1987

Grateful acknowledgment is made for permission to reprint:
"Reprobate", which originally appeared in *Black American Literature Forum*, and
"Universal", which originally appeared in Ishmael Reed and Al Young's *Quilt IV.*

Published by Precedent Publishing, Inc.
770 N. LaSalle Street
Chicago, Illinois 60610
Manufactured in U.S.A.

2nd Printing, 1998

Library of Congress Cataloging-in-Publication Data

Stuckey, Elma, 1907 –
   The collected poems of Elma Stuckey

   I. Hirsch, E.D. (Eric Donald), 1926 –
PS3569.T83A17   1987   811'.54   87-3532
ISBN 0-9667548-04-8

Contents

Introduction to The Collected Poems

This moving, often humorous collection of
poems shows again that Elma Stuckey belongs
among the authentic American poets of our cen-
tury. Extending the scope and variety of her dis-
tinguished earlier book, *The Big Gate* (1976), this
new collection of poems will once again delight
those readers who have already come to know
Elma Stuckey's poetry, and will be a happy rev-
elation to those readers who are not yet ac-
quainted with it. The publication of this book ten
years after the publication of *The Big Gate* now
establishes Elma Stuckey in the canon of modern
American poetry.

Elma Stuckey was born in Memphis, Tennes-
see, in 1907. Her grandfather was an ex-slave. In
her childhood neighborhood in North Memphis
there still lived a number of ex-slaves. Her close-
ness to the authentic lore and victorious, biting
humor of slave culture provided her with a
major theme of *The Big Gate*. The big gate was a
place, out of hearing of the masters, where slaves
could exchange confidences and tell stories, and
achieve within the world of words and imagina-
tion a dignity and consolation denied them in the
world of brute fact. Humor, religious faith, and
biting satire were the staples of their exchanges,
and these tones made up the dominant tenor of
Elma Stuckey's earlier volume. Now those same
themes and tones are continued in this new book,
but they are deepened, and are interspersed with
more contemporary, yet equally universal
themes.

How did Elma Stuckey become such an accomplished poet? The ultimate answer to such a question must always remain a secret. Poets, Horace tells us, are born, not made. But even born poets need encouragement, and that encouragement Elma Stuckey received from her family. When she was eleven, her father, a successful businessman in Memphis, gave her a book of poems, and throughout her childhood her father and mother supported her natural talent for speaking poetry at social gatherings, where she often recited poems of her own making. As her local reputation grew, she was frequently asked to compose poems for special occasions.

There were other ways in which Elma Stuckey was fortunate in her family. She was fortunate in their enterprise, public spirit, and respect for learning. She graduated from a Memphis high school that was co-founded by her father. She spent two years at Lane College in Jackson, Tennessee, an institution that had been founded by Bishop Lane, a relative. But it was not just her family's encouragement and high values that caused Elma Stuckey to become a true poet. It was her own insight, talent, and strength of character that made her a figure of spiritual authority both within her family and outside it, a sage and a poet at once.

These poems need no elaborate introductory explanations. They speak eloquently for themselves. Any reader who is knowing in the complexities of the human heart will grasp them at once. Yet it will not be out of place to mention some characteristics of Elma Stuckey's poems that are particularly dear to me. It happens that in some of her ballad-like poems Elma Stuckey

shares a wonderful spiritual affinity with my
favorite poet, William Blake. As just one
example of that affinity consider the following:

> If I am blind and need someone
> To keep me safe from harm,
> It matters not the race to me
> Of the one who takes my arm.
>
> For mercy has a human heart,
> Pity a human face,
> And love the human form divine
> And peace the human dress.
>
> And all must love the human form,
> In heathen, Turk or Jew;
> Where mercy, love, and pity dwell
> There God is dwelling too.

The first stanza is by Elma Stuckey, the second
and third by Blake. Why do they fit together so
perfectly in form, theme, and diction? Not
because Elma Stuckey was influenced by Blake;
that is unlikely. It is because they both build
upon the strengths of the ballad form, and the
power of an apparent simplicity that resonates
within a deeply complex religious tradition.
But neither Blake nor Elma Stuckey conveys a
tame religious vision. Just as Blake delighted in
both the Lamb and the Tiger, so Elma Stuckey
delights in vigorous badness as well as vigorous
goodness in the human heart. Both kinds of vigor
are associated with the divine spark of vitality.
What a contrast there is between "If I am blind
and need someone" and "Tate":

> Ya'll know the reason
> I follow Tate around?
> 'Cause I like to smell his breath,
> It's so full of whiskey.

To Elma Stuckey, a woman who loves a bad
man *despite* his badness is not as interesting as a
woman who loves a man *because* of the badness
that expresses his vitality.

Nowhere is Elma Stuckey's positive feeling for
strong personalities more shockingly realized
than in the poem "Sacrilegious," about a char-
acter who is strong-mindedly (and divinely) vital
enough to scorn Jesus:

> "There's one thing He never counted on,
> When He was leading His flock.
> Lil' ole sissy, letting men kiss Him,
> Well, Judas fixed His clock."

The connections of vitality, strong-
mindedness, unconventionality, and sexual drive
with something miraculous or divine come out
brilliantly in "Lill."

> Lill was lying paralyzed
> On her left side.
> Before I could say a word,
> She ordered me to take a tissue off the top
> Of a kleenex box,
> To lay aside a pork sandwich
> And to take a half-pint of whiskey
> From the bottom of the box.

After she drinks the whiskey, Lill asserts her
continued sexual attractiveness and potency, and
the poem ends:

> Eventually she walked out of the hospital
> As well as anyone:
> What led her to walk again
> Is a question that boggles my mind.
> Was it the pork or whiskey
> Or was it the two combined?

4

The themes I have mentioned merely touch the surface of these remarkable poems. Perhaps the most powerful poems of the collection are the character studies. One of them, the major work which gives the second book its name, "Ribbons and Lace," is a masterpiece that should find its way into standard anthologies of American poetry. The subject of this long poem is Aint Rachel, an ex-slave and midwife (and infidel!), who embodies the dark, irrational powers of both nature and the human soul.

We must be grateful to Elma Stuckey for so much richness and delight. Without further preamble I invite the reader to taste these riches.

E.D. Hirsch, Jr.
Kenan Professor of English
The University of Virginia

THE BIG GATE

*To my daughter and son
Jean and Sterling*

Introduction

One of the most rewarding experiences in the study and evaluation of literature is the discovery of a writer of significant talent who deserves to be better known. Elma Stuckey is such a writer. She is almost sixty-nine years old and has been writing poetry since her teens but her work, which has appeared in some half-dozen journals, is not well known.

The Big Gate, Elma Stuckey's first book of poems, is passionately felt and skillfully rendered. Like many Afro-American poets, she draws upon two traditions, the literary and the folk, both of which she handles well, but the latter with a special verve and insight which distinguish her from other writers in this vein. Her subject is no less than the revolutionary spirit implicit in the actions of the ordinary men and women who kept their humanity intact under the oppression of slavery and segregation.

The poet is the mother of Sterling Stuckey, the young historian whose seminal essay, "Through the Prism of Folklore: The Black Ethos in Slavery," in *The Massachusetts Review*, helped set the tone and direction of recent scholarship on the subject. Reading the poems, one immediately perceives the intellectual and spiritual bond between mother and son. Even more important, however, is the wider tradition, the larger continuity. These poems were *inspired* by Mrs. Stuckey's recollections of the ex-slaves in her community of North Memphis, Tennessee, where she lived until her mid-thirties. She thus serves an important role in the transmitting of this knowledge. More important still is the distillation and interpretation of experience which her art has produced. With the exception of Dunbar, Elma Stuckey probably devotes more attention to slavery than any other poet, certainly more than any other living poet. She does not write "Dunbars," however, as poems in the tradition of Paul Lawrence Dunbar are sometimes called. She is closer in style and tone to Sterling Brown, though to be more accurate, one should say, to the realistic apprehension of the folk life and lore and art which characterizes his work. Nevertheless, the period with which she mainly deals is not the '20s and '30s of Brown's, but that of enslavement itself.

The poems in black vernacular are especially important for their variety, and for their treatment of themes current in black oral tradition but rarely set down in writing, especially in poetry. These include sexual relations between master, mistress and slave, and realistic self-portraits of black drivers, traitors, Toms, and Sambos. They include ironic and cynical attitudes toward God, as in "Long Cotton Row" and "Jim," who "got a crow for to pick with God." There is delicious humor in "Beulah," who resists her master's advances, and "Sally," with her special recipe for okra soup.

There are the common humanity and human frailty of "Emancipation Proclamation" and of "Lettie," whose "Ole Missus was as po' as me/ And both of us dipped snuff." There are lovely lyrics like "Traveling Light," and "Cracked Saucer," a commonplace object that is a quiet and moving metaphor of the human condition.

The post-slavery poems are also notable for

their variety. Some of the portraits are sharp and bluesy, as in "An Egg in Each Basket:" "Gotta stay on the good side/of the devil and with God,/Don't know which one I end up with/When they put me in the sod." Contrasted with that picture of honesty are the religious hypocrites and gulls, as in "Jackleg," "Timing" and "Feeding the Pastor," all too familiar figures of black life.

One finds among the "literary" poems the delightful word play of "Rigmarole: Puzzles for Children," the eloquent "For W. E. B. Du Bois," and the apocalyptic vision of the Last Judgment in the charging rhythm and virtuoso rhyming of "Trumpet."

Some of these poems should be read aloud, for their inner shape comes from an oral tradition which sometimes can only be suggested on the page. That is the way I first heard them: from Elma Stuckey's vital voice. Her voice comes alive in these lines. Read them and hear it. Hear it and hear the voices of the people who created the spirituals and the blues.

Stephen E. Henderson

Jim

He's gonna chop his way into Heaven,
He was buried with the hoe in his hand,
And he knows just how to swing it
'cause Jim was a cotton choppin' man.

Now Jim was big and powerful,
Yeah, Jim was a six-foot man,
He's gonna chop the door wide open,
Means to get in the promised land.

Old Jim didn't say no prayers,
Bare-foot he sung them blues,
He don't like no milk and honey,
Won't wear no silvery shoes.

He swo' when he chopped the cotton,
He swo' cause he worked so hard,
Old Jim had a tough time livin',
He got a crow for to pick with God.

He's sho gonna get into Heaven,
He was buried with the hoe in his hand,
And he knows just how to swing it
'cause Jim was a cotton choppin' man.

Boy

I'se eighty year old and my name is Boy,
Ain't had no fun, but I'se had joy,
Had my joy when Marsa died,
When I moaned and wailed and laughed inside.

Lettie

Sure slavery time was rough
On our plantation, tough!
Ole Missus was as poor as me
And both of us dipped snuff.

Long Cotton Row

Lord, don't set that sun
On the long cotton row,
Look like I done chopped
'til I can't chop no mo'.

Shoo that sun over there
Right behind that cloud,
Then when breeze come 'long
I be mighty proud.

That'll make the day mo' easy,
Won't seem so long gettin' through,
And if I ain't too broken down
I'll sho be praisin' You,
That's if I ain't too broken down. . .

No Wings

I hear a wagon rumbling far away,
It's going somewhere but I'm here to stay,
Ain't got no wings so I can't fly,
If I get 'em be by-and-by

Burying Ground

One o' these days I lay cotton sack down,
I be ready for the buryin' ground.
Yeah, one o' these days I lay cotton sack down,
Go on to heaven and get my crown.

Ole Marse has got a pointed nose,
He got a pointed chin,
Ain't got no lips but just a slit,
He look like homemade sin.

The cracks is crisscross on his neck
And he baldheaded too,
He mad 'cause he been white so long
And still ain't well-to-do.

He don't look like he human,
You can't tell front from back,
That man, he am so mis'able
I b'lieve he wish he black.

I'm glad Marse give me driver job,
It make me feel just fine,
He say to me, "You nigger you,
You keep the slaves in line."

He beat the slaves so awful,
Once that included me,
But now I beat 'em for Ole Marse,
I feel I'm just 'bout free.

House Niggers

Two times they call us from the field
And tell us Marse is dying,
Two times house niggers huddle up
And all of them is crying.

I'se sick of looking at that sight
And ask them why they cry,
They say they tired of waiting,
Marse take too long to die.

The Big Gate

Slaves often stood out of earshot of
the master, down at the gate to the path leading
to the great house, and told
tall tales. . . .

I

We's gathered here to tell our tales
'bout how we treat Ole Marse,
Some tales be big, some tales be small,
Sometimes the tales be sparse.

II

First of all I tell my tale.
None of you was 'round
When I pick up my fist and say,
"I'll knock you to the ground."

I say, "Old Marse, I owns you,
You knows that you is mine."
That man, he whimper like a dog,
Ain't nothin' in his spine.

Now if Ole Marse come up here
To raise hell like the dickens,
I'll chase him right between you all
And scatter you like chickens.

III

There ain't no Marse can trick me,
I'se always on the ball,
I take my fist and knock 'em dead
And don't care where they fall.

Last one I whupped, here come Miss,
She say, "Marse on the flo'!
What happen' to your Marsa?
Don't say that you don't know."

I say, "Ole Miss, I do my work
Like you done told me to,
I call you when I see him fall,
What else I s'pose to do?"

IV

I'm stuck wid Marse, he stuck wid me.
He tried to sell me twice,
The traders say, "Hell no, not Bose,
Not Bose at any price."

The secret is, I'se on the block
And so I thumbs my nose.
Marse do not see but traders see,
That's why they don't want Bose.

V

Shucks, I ain't scared o' Marse,
I treat him like a snake.
I twist his neck and stomp his tail
And curl him 'round my rake.

I talks to him like I is boss
And talk like he is slave.
If any Tom is at this gate
I put him in his grave.

VI

Ole Miss' tell Marse to beat me!
I is in puzzlement.
She knows I is de mean one,
Ain't broken and ain't bent.

I run smack-dab into dat man
And choke 'im like de devil,
Ole Missus look and clap de hands,
Say, "Boys, go git de shovel!"

VII

We s'pose to listen at this gate
But no one's heard me yet.
I got a tale to beat all tales—
Don' b'lieve me? What you bet?

I kilt Ole Marse and buried him—
You think I lie? I ain't—
If you see somethin' look like Marse
Just pay no mind, that's haint.

VIII

From miles around they knowed me,
Plantation to plantation.
I is most stubborn slave of all,
I'se hell and all damnation.

Nobody rule this brawny man,
Nobody try to whip 'im.
If S.O.B. stand up to me
I sho' to hell will lick 'im.

I'se bad, real bad, Marse knows I'se bad,
Bet you don't see 'im comin',
And if you see Ole Marse at all
You see his back, he runnin'.

IX

Look folks, pay me some 'tention
'bout what I got to say,
Y'all just so glad that Marse is dead
And buried yesterday.

Nobody ask one question,
What kilt him, made him sick?
Since you ain't ask, I shut my mouth
'bout why he died so quick.

X

I'se wishin' I could drown Ole Marse,
He plays into my hand,
Come at me when I'm fishin'
And come er-raisin' sand.

We grapple and we struggle,
We hit the river bed,
We down there where no one can see
And so I push his head.

Now that's the last I seen of him,
Don't blame no mess on me
Because I swim up to the top
And he float out to sea.

XI

Marse give us head, he give us tail
And then he give us middlins,
He give us ears, he give us feet
And then he give us chittlins.

I slip and burn the smoke house down,
Ole Marse rage and cuss,
He knowed we et the hams and ribs
that done been cooked for us.

XII

Had three Marsas in my time,
Each one was scared of me,
But being white they had to bluff
'cause other slaves would see.

They knew they could not whip me
But each just had to try,
And I done warned, "You lift that whip,
You kiss this world goodbye."

They raised the whip, I kept my word,
They never lay a lick on me,
I betcha you can find three graves
And I ain't on no tree.

XIII

Little bit of lye each day
Stirred easy in his whiskey.
Now he am in de family plot,
That way it were not risky.

XIV

Ole Marse would whup me in de field,
He says I is de lazies',
I smart 'nough to choke him good
And now he pushin' daisies.

XV

My trouble were not with Ole Marse,
It were with Marsa's Missis.
She make me climb in bed with her
And say it bettern' his is.

XVI

Hot weather come, I fan that man
'til he drop off to sleep.
I scratch my head and figure how
To make his sleep be deep.

I gather up some poison weeds
And beat them into dust,
And fan it close while he am sleep
And that am fair and just.

One night that dust hit home on him,
He did not cough or hack,
But keeled and died with crooked neck,
Doc called it heart attack.

XVII

I sing and dance for my Old Marse,
I holler and I whoop,
He think I happy and I is
'bout to fly the coop.

XVIII

Ole Marse, he had stud nigger,
Dat nigger hit de lick!
Ole Missus heard about him
And now she big as tick.

XIX

I put spiders in the pot,
Black widows to be sho'
They et and praise me highly,
I'se glad to see them go.

XX

I goes up to the big house
Before Ole Missus rise,
I stand right over Missus' bed
And catch her by surprise.

I say, "Git up, you lazy thing,
Git up and cook for me."
She buck her eyes 'til they pop out,
So scared she cannot see.

I tell her, "You no mo' Miss Anne,
To me you plain old Annie.
Call me Miss Lue and do it quick
Or else I whip your fannie."

She say, "I'm white and I can't cook,
My white lips can't say Miss."
I say "I slap you side your head—
Now you take that and this!"

Here come Ole Marse from other room,
"Miss Lue, if what I see
Is that you slap old Annie's face,
Hit one more lick for me."

XXI

Saint Peter tell me watch his gate,
Don't let no bad 'uns in,
And so I put my hands on hips
To stop each one that sin.

I see Ole Marsa treckin' 'long,
He trudgin' up the line,
And so I says unto myself,
At last your meat is mine.

He at the gate, he see me there,
He rear way back and swell,
I slam that gate and say to him,
"You git the hell to hell!"

XXII

Everyone done told a tale,
The last tale fall on me,
I got no right talking here
'cause y'all know I'se free.

I sho' don't chop no cotton
And I don't pick none too,
Marsa is so scared of me
I is the "Booger Boo."

I goes this way and that way
And never need no pass,
Ole Marse look down, cap in hand,
He know he bet' not sass.

Marse a lush head son of a gun,
I just now caught him plastered.
Go on y'all, lay in the shade,
'cause I done kilt the bastard.

I Been There

My body is weak and sickly
But it done served Marse well,
I'se gonna land in heaven,
Already been through hell.

No matter what folks say,
My Marse was kind to me,
Kind enough to up and die
And that's what set me free.

Runaway

I run away from beatin'
And just can't understan'
Why a slave that git beat too
Can tell on other man.

I'se skulkin' in the bushes
And climb up in a tree,
I know a slave done told Marse
'zackly where I be.

I'se hungry and done got weak,
Cone pone would be a feast.
It am a shame Marse stalkin' me,
He am the one the beast.

Mystery

One thing sure do shock me,
I seen Marse on his knees.
They say Ole Marse was praying,
Explain that if you please.

Shepherd

Folks think I talking to myself,
I talking to my God
'bout if the devil come too close
To poke him with His rod.

Hallelujah

I'm gonna shout, oh yes I am,
And jump up straight and down,
Back away, get a running start
When God hold up my crown

Mother and Child

Every night I dream about
Ole Marse selling my child,
I scream and holler in my sleep,
They claim that I am wild.

Don't know where she is today,
My baby was just three.
What kind of mamma would I be
If it don't worry me.

Call me crazy, call me touched,
And you can say I'm wild,
But remember it all started
When Marsa sold my child.

Sundown

The sun's goin' down, heavenly Lord,
And I go right behind it.
Cover my track, heavenly Lord,
And Ole Marse never find it.

Hezekiah

I rec'lect the driver man
Was sleeping very sound.
That's when I snuck up on him,
Now he am in the ground.

Ole Marse never caught me
But he was in a huff.
That is all, for that is that—
Fetch me my box of snuff.

Jenny

Ole Missus were a sorry sight,
She knowed that I knowed too,
Ole Marsa ran from shack to shack
Like all Ole Marsas do.

Rebel

I break the hoe, I break the plow
And here he come, that hellion.
I say right then unto myself,
This a one-man rebellion.

I stand foursquare and face Ole Marse,
He call me crazy nigger,
I rush him and I take his gun
And then I pull the trigger.

My time is come and I don't care
If they hang me from a tree,
By bein' crazy like a fox
I sent Marse 'head of me.

He bowed and scraped and loved Ole Marse,
A grovelin' black slave nigger,
And after pizenin' Ole Marse
A shufflin' black grave digger.

I seen 'em whipped and branded too,
And strung up in the trees,
I seen a-many baby sold,
Ole Marse do what he please.

My head is full of Marsa's scars,
My back is full of stripes,
And I am even branded too,
But I wiped out my gripes.

I took my chance and grabbed his gun
And held it very steady,
Blowed off his head, I got to run—
They look for me already.

Remember

The doctor say Marse' mind is sound,
That it is wide awake,
And say when Marsa draw last breath
Then that will free old Jake.

So everything am settled now,
The lawyer heard 'im too,
But I hear something else speak out:
Say, Jake, what you gon' do?

You sho' has been good servant,
You served for thirty years,
You 'member when he sold your child
And you was full of tears?

46

Sissy

I won't let Marsa pat me jes'
Because I'm big and plump.
Ole Missus, she is straight up down,
Ain't nowhere is a bump.

Marse shake the sheet to find her
To see if she in bed,
She there alright, but she don't move,
She stiff jes' like she dead.

Ole Marse look at de pallet,
Say "Lucius, 'member me?
Look, Lucius, at your Marsa,
You live, I set you free."

Old Lucius say, "My eyes is dim,
I know it's Marsa's voice,
But death don't lie when he am come,
I make old death my choice."

Rebuked

Y'all talkin' crazy when yer ask
A man like me that's black
Why I let Marsa beat me
And put marks on my back.

I was not scared, the point I make,
You see, I was not free,
No more than one o' Marsa's mules,
Don't be so hard on me.

Old King Cotton

Oh yeah, I know they call you King
And how you make their pockets ring,
You've really been a trying thing,
Old King Cotton,

You saw me up and down the row
Chopping grass with sharpened hoe,
Pulling weeds to help you grow,
Old King Cotton,

You saw my old black woman too
And all the things she did for you,
You saw our chillun scamper through,
Old King Cotton,

You saw them melons on the vine,
Saw me bust one many a time
And pass a chunk on down the line,
Old King Cotton,

You know that old grey mule, I bet,
How he would balk and I would fret,
But plowed until the sun did set,
Old King Cotton,

You saw me when I laid you by
And looked you over with my eye,
I said you'd bring a price that's high,
Old King Cotton,

We gonna start you ginning through,
Bless my soul, you'll see that too,
And you will hear me say to you,
Rotten, rotten cotton.

He swore that he would not be whipped
Or trot at beck and call,
Ole Marsa screamed, "I'll break you in,
I'll beat you 'til you crawl."

He grabbed Ole Marsa by the neck
And headed for the well
And jumping in he hollered back,
"Me an' Ole Marse eat supper in hell!"

Selling Melvina

"What bid do I hear for this comely wench?
You have seen her buttocks and bust.
She's as ripe as the fallen fruit, you see.
What do I hear? Bid on your lust."

"Five hundred I bid for that black heifer."
"By Jove, I will make it seven.
I have got to own that nigger wench,
I swear by Hell and all Heaven."

Melvina was chewing a poison leaf
And stood like a statue of stone,
The auctioneer called, "Going, going. . .
She's toppled — Hell! She's gone."

Upstart

Young Marse, you come to beat me
And say don't give no lip,
But I can't work cause rheumatiz
Is got me in the hip.

Last lickin like to kilt me,
I waits for God right now,
Tha's why I has to speak my mind
Tho' you beat me anyhow.

Ole Missus made me nurse you first,
Then my black breast stopped givin',
My baby died, you got the milk,
One reason you is livin'.

He pray, he sing, he shout and cry
And that am every Sunday,
Next thing we know, Marse whippin' us
And that am every Monday.

Duke

Marse shot the ground around his feet
To make him jig and leap,
But now he jig on Marsa's grave
So glad Marse six foot deep.

Sally

She clear her throat and spit in soup
And do it three, four time.
She throw some okra in the pot,
That too will make a slime.

Ole Marsa slop it up like hog:
"Sally, by jove, it's good!"
And Sally say, "I sure is glad,
I done the best I could."

Tom

I lay my head on choppin' block,
To Marsa I is true.
To all the niggers call me Tom,
Ole Marse is white, is you?

I hold his hat, his walkin' stick
And help him wid his coat,
And when I sin he slap my back
And say, "You doggone goat!"

I like to git that praise from Marse,
His praise is mighty slim,
And when he call me doggone goat
That's pet name come from him.

I slink around and tell Ole Marse
The secrets of the niggers,
And when I tell he kick me well,
I don't know how that figgers.

I flunky 'round and serves him
His brandy and his gin,
And when I do he take his cane
And whack me on the shin.

I look at him, I'se grinnin',
He look at me rat grim,
He knows I is good nigger,
Tell me, wha's wrong wid him?

Southern Belle

Ole Missus is a vile one,
Got everything, she rich!
But walk around house niggers
Buck naked, not a stitch.

I don't know what she provin',
Ole Marsa love the shacks,
There's something in them quarters
That his Ole Missus lacks.

Leora

They say they can't control me
And say I never happy.
How can I be when I know he,
Ole Marsa, is my pappy.

Jane

'scuse me, white folks, I'se old and dull,
Two things I does remember,
My name is Jane, I chopped Ole Marse,
I think it in December

Pete

Ole Marsa's wife done run away,
She leave him all a-sudden,
He mad as hell 'cause he done looked
And he can't find nare nudden.

Beulah

Ole Marse, he throw me on the bed
And so I fights, 'cause I is scared,
I kicks him where his trouble is,
Mine's alright, he nursin' his.

To get my freedom I would chance my life,
But I ain't running and leaving my wife.
I had a chance just yesterday,
Could have been gone far away.

Ole Marse was drunk and the driver man too,
Neither was watching as they always do.
But I'll stick out this lowly life,
I ain't running and leaving my wife.

Posted

I

Two mules for sale and one black boy,
He's strong and very big,
Now if you buy the lot of them
I'll throw in one fat pig.

II

I'm overloaded, got too much,
Niggers, chickens, hogs, and such,
Donkeys, mules, turkeys too,
This is the sale I offer you.

III

Tacked on a tree a great big sign,
"Looking for a sire?
Come and see this burly black
I have got for hire."

IV

Look out for Carrie, she's not fat,
Just showing what she's done,
So if you find her rush her back,
Reward is one for one.

V

Catch young Lindy, she looks like white,
But just another black,
Talks real smart, calls me "Damn Pa"
They say, behind my back.

VI

A black boy, George, 'bout twenty-five,
A rascal, scoundrel too,
He runs away 'bout once a month,
So I am warning you

He is a dangerous nigger,
The kind you just can't case,
He holds his cap and keeps a grin
That spreads across his face.

VII

Don't judge my nigger by his mouth,
He's young and he is stout,
The reason that he lost some teeth
Is 'cause I knocked 'em out.

VIII

Ole Lonnie is a runaway.
I greased him up real good
And put some polish on his head
To sell him if I could.

You catch that nigger, wash his head
To see if it is gray,
You know right then he is my boy—
Don't let him get away.

So much I hates 'bout slavery time,
Some things I hasn't tell,
But now I know Old Marse is dead
And burnin' down in hell.

Come creepin' in my cabin,
Done sold my man away,
And fumble 'round half 'o de night
And sneak out just 'fore day.

Ole Missus 'tend she do not know,
Head up and dressed up fine,
One thing I know she do not know,
I fed Ole Marse strychnine.

Mandy

Ole Marse is potbelly man,
Dat man can't see de feet,
Come sidlin' up real close to me
Like he am in de heat.

He puff and blow and then he say,
"You wench, I goin' to grind it!"
I step aside and laugh at him,
I know he never find it.

Preacher Man

White preacher like a mangy dog,
Each time he turn around
The dandruff fall from off his head
And flutter to the ground.

He preach straight to the white folks,
Sometime he turn aside
And tell us slaves that's squattin' there,
"Let Marsa tan your hide."

"You take your beatin' like a slave,
Obey and don't fight back,
You know your Marsa owns you,
You know he's white, you black."

Obey, obey, that's all I hear,
So I obeyed my mind
And when the preachin' over with
I creep up close behind.

Now ain't no flaky dandruff
Come fallin' from his head
'cause he ain't standin' up no mo',
He stretched out and he dead.

Lou had to leave her sickly child
To sit with Missus' naughty boy
Who cut many a caper
And played with every toy.

When Missus finally came home
Lou wrapped a shawl around her head,
Then went into her cabin
To find her baby dead.

Rain

Sunshine days Ole Marsa nice,
He laugh wid us and joke,
But let dere come a rainy day
Ole Marsa break his yoke.

He trot just like a bloodhound
And run from hut to cabin
To find black woman all alone
And try to start to dabbin'.

Traveling Light

Gonna knock off early Saturday night,
Walk for miles in the cool moonlight,
Get there soon 'cause my feet be light,
See my wife and be all right.

I holler hallelujah,
I jump up and I shout,
Ain't gettin' on my knees no more,
Done just 'bout wore 'em out.

Things go 'long about the same,
I try to do what's right,
I can't please Marse and can't please God,
I reckon He is white.

I always prayed to the Lord
That things be turned about,
Ain't gettin' on my knees no more,
Done just 'bout wore 'em out.

Seed Abe Lincum wid my eyes,
He travelin' through the lan',
Know what else my eyes do see?
He one mo' ugly man.

His only slave freed and gone,
Red-necked cracker all alone,
No crop to plant, no crop to reap,
All his troubles piled so steep.

Barefoot, ragged, hurting, sick,
Just a meat skin now to lick.
Stomach empty, tightened belt,
Hunger's for niggers, so he felt.

"Boy," he said, "you damn' old black,
Out of my sight and don't come back.
Don't want your food, out of my sight!
I'm clinging to this—I'm white, I'm white!"

My bones a-creakin' on a creaky bed,
No soft place for to lay my head,
One day good Lord gonna lay me down,
Soft, soft sleepin' under the ground.

Movin' Nowhere

I keep on movin', ain't gettin' nowhere,
Plow from here and down to there,
Start again from here to there,
I keep on movin', ain't gettin' nowhere.

Cracked Saucer

My saucer done cracked
And my coffee's gone,
Got nothin' ter wash down
The cold cone pone

Old crack so tricky
Let it leak out slow,
Didn't see my coffee
When it started to go

My saucer done cracked
My coffee done gone,
Nothin' to wash down
The cold cone pone

The Vision

I've seen heaven, children,
While lying in my bed
Golden gates flew open,
A light shined on my head

I saw angels flying
With glitter on their wings,
It almost blinded me
To see such pretty things

I've seen heaven, children,
And I'll be there for sure
On that great getting up day
Because my heart is pure

For Aubrie

His Hands

They told the story better
Than anything he could ever say.
They were a loving symbol
Of his life from day to day.

To them no man was stranger
As they gave to those in need.
They were eager to share his earnings,
Had never known the thing called greed.

They lifted heavy timber,
Worked with stone and mortar, dug clay,
Yet gently held the baby
At the close of some hard day.

They held his Bible firmly,
Turning slowly page by page.
They were devout and constant,
And never struck in rage.

They did not know the manicurist's touch
Or glisten with jewels set in rings.
They were adorned with creases and careworn,
And only dealt in honest things.

How well I know they labored
From sun-up 'til eventide.
His hands were so willing,
As if an unseen censor their guide.

The last time I saw them, may God have mercy,
They were folded across his breast.
Though Papa will live eternally,
May his hands forever rest.

Timing

Now and then she would shout in church,
Walking down the aisle,
With one hand raised toward heaven,
Screaming all the while.

She wanted to be seen
When she was all decked out,
When wearing a new dress or hat
Was the only time she'd shout.

Mourners Bench

The sinners were coaxed to sit up front.
There were gamblers and a wench,
There were whoremongers and drunkards
And backsliders on the bench.

The preacher sweated and hollered,
"He'll forgive, don't care what you do.
Just trust Him tonight, Oh trust Him,
For Jesus loves all of you."

He screamed, "Trust in Jesus,
Just listen to His teaching."
Those on the bench were saved
By his pleading and his preaching.

The wench went right back to whoring,
The gamblers went right back to gambling,
The drunkard went right back to drinking,
The whoremonger right back to rambling.

They all had one thing in common,
They felt they had nothing to fear.
They'd keep on sinning since He forgives,
And return to the bench next year.

I just can't put all my trust
In a fella I ain't seen,
I don't know whether He's friendly,
I don't know whether He's mean.

Now there's that other fella,
The one they say is so bad.
If I should crack a joke for him,
Could be the best laugh he's had.

Gotta stay on the good side
Of the devil and with God,
Don't know which one I land up with
When they put me in the sod.

Old Man

Old man, you ain't always been good
And doing all the things you should,
I bet you did everything you could,
Long time ago,

Now, you ain't been good all your life,
I bet you danced to fiddle and fife
And s'peck you used to beat your wife,
Long time ago,

Now you try to give advice,
The things you say sound just too nice.
Say, didn't you used to shoot them dice,
Long time ago?

Now you've got a pious look,
Just as if you wouldn't crook.
Whose wife was it that you took,
Long time ago?

Go on, old man, and play your role,
I ain't gonna tell it to a soul,
But God done wrote it on His scroll
A long time ago.

Jackleg

"Sinners, gamblers, whores and such,
Come off from that back row,
Come to the front and tell the Lord
To make the devil go.

"Come ye brethren, come up close
And come ye sisters too.
But don't you sisters get too close,
No telling what I do."

She emptied her purse on the table
'cause the preacher had called her honey.
She went on home satisfied
Though she had no insurance money.

She caught a chicken and wrung its neck,
She had already cooked a roast,
But she wanted to load the table
So he could eat and boast.

The pastor came right on time
And headed for the table,
He tucked a napkin under his chin
And ate what he was able.

He drove away in a cadillac
Like so many black preachers do,
Since she was good at wringing necks
She should have wrung his too.

She was black and sold moonshine
For a white man she called Joe,
She was a bootleg woman,
Yeah, she was that for sho'.

She had a daughter, name of Lil,
And the night that mamma died
Lil took a swig of moonshine
And they say she never cried,
They say she never cried.

She got on the phone and talked to Joe,
"Have you heard that mamma's dead?
Bring two gallons of moonshine—
One for the foot of the casket
And one for to set at the head,
Yeah, one for the foot of the casket
And one for to set at the head."

And Joe brought the moonshine,
Two gallons, like Lil said,
One for the foot of the casket
And one for to set at the head,
Yeah, one for the foot of the casket
And one for to set at the head.

Gambler

He lived so recklessly that
His mamma told him, "Son,
If you never mend your ways
You'll die with your shoes on,
Die with your shoes on."

He kept on shooting dice
And not once did he pray,
Though seldom was he lucky
He continued anyway.

That he tried with loaded dice
The gamblers had no doubt,
He shook the dice and rolled them,
And then a shot rang out.

He screamed, "Come take off my shoes,"
Knowing that he would die,
"I wanna make mamma out
A low-down Goddamn lie,
Low-down Goddamn lie."

Let Them Come

Let them come
As they usually do by night
With eyes of blue steel
And hearts of stone,

Let them come
As they usually do in throngs
With whiskey breath and
Tobacco dripping mouths
To take one black,

Let them wait
As they usually do
Squatting on haunches
Lusting for blood,

Let them come, let them come,
Not a one would dare
Come alone.

Cannonball

I worked this strip to make the railroad track,
I grunted umph, umph, cross ties on my back,
I know the railroad and how it was built,
I know 'bout the black men the railroad kilt.

A train can't run unless it got a track.
I toted that shining steel on my back.
Yeah, I laid them ties and I drove the spike
When they started the railroad through this pike.

The train blow for the crossing, slowing down,
Don't want for to stop in this little town.
I hear them wheels going clickety clack,
It seems to me it's ridin' on my back.

I'm all bent over from toting the steel.
The train moves through like a long, long eel.
It's highballing through to hit the big town.
If you gonna ride, better flag it down.

Yeah, it pass this town like it don't exist.
I don't wave at the train, I shake my fist.
I ain't got no money and I can't ride,
But I laid them tracks and I got my pride.

For Ossie Davis and Ruby Dee

Little Boys

"Little white boy, when you grow up,
What do you want to be?"
"Oh, doctor, lawyer, or president,
It is all left up to me."

"Little black boy, when you grow up,
What will you be, tell me?"
"You asking me, a little black boy?
I be plain lucky to be."

Some folks can live while others die,
Some folks can laugh while others cry,
Some places are far and some are nigh,
Some folks like cake and others pie,
There's a low for every high,
Sometimes I wonder why.

Well, there's a this for every that,
And there's a tit for every tat,
You got to sit before you've sat,
And there's a chit for every chat,
You got to spit before you've spat,
If that's not true I'll eat my hat.

If there's a criss, well there's a cross,
And something found was something lost,
Some things are free while others cost,
Some ride a mule, some ride a hoss,
A rolling stone don't catch no moss,
You work for me, that makes me boss.

Some roads are crooked, some are straight,
Some don't eat much, some clean the plate,
Some folks are early and some are late,
Some get in soon while others wait,
You call it luck, I call it fate,
You go through cracks, I find the gate.

Some folks got hair, some wear a wig,
Some dance the waltz, some do a jig,
Some things zag and some things zig,
Some are little and some are big,
Some get it easy while others dig,
I got my cow, you got your pig.

Here is rain and there is dew,
Here am I and there are you,
You are one, we both make two,
There is old and there is new,
Some things we fry and some things stew,
I don't know, I wish I knew. . .

The land is dry, the river wet,
Some babies cry and others fret,
Some folks perspire while others sweat,
Some doors are open, others shet,
I feel the wind, ain't seen it yet,
Now just how silly can this get?

There's a smile for every frown,
If I'm a fool then you're a clown,
If this is up, then that is down,
If this is square, then that is round,
Some folks swim and others drown,
I know how crazy all this sounds!

For Ella Jenkins

Daylight Saving Time

Some folks are getting mighty smart
In every kind of way,
Some Alec done got too smart
And changed the time of day.

This time has got us mesmerized,
It gets us up too soon,
And then we have to go to bed
'bout time we see the moon.

Setting all the clocks ahead,
Messing up the town,
And changing this and changing that
Done run it in the groun'.

Trying to make that sun wait—
That sun don't tell no lies,
Folks better stay in folks' place,
And quit messing with the skies.

God's gonna come riding through
And raging in his wrath,
Gonna strike down everybody
That happens in his path.

You gonna ask the Lord to wait
So you can change His mind,
And God's gonna say, "Man, I can't wait,
I come on Daylight Saving Time."

Stop sending duns to my house.
Them bills is Phillip's bills.
I told you he don't live here.
Phillip is in the hills.

He left here in November,
He ain't been back no mo',
Phillip's got a new address
Where the wild flowers grow.

His address is in a graveyard—
Which one? You look about,
I don't tell The Man
Where Phillip's hiding out.

News

Guess I'll go on down to the newsstand
And tell Isaiah Mack is dead.
Mack, who went every day to buy the paper,
Talking with Isaiah about the headlines
And the editorials and obituaries,
The ones that's gone.

Two old cronies
Who got many a laugh over the society pages,
The pictures of ladies and gentlemen
All in evening gowns and tux and ties.
Mack's death didn't make the paper,
So I'll go down and let Isaiah know
Mack won't be coming 'round no more.

For W. E. B. Du Bois

Now the fragrant petals shower downward
That hung suspended in an air of fear,
But he is gone and now they fall resplendent
In solemn reverence for that mighty seer.

That great exponent of the freedom surge
Who advocated that the black man fight,
Whose dreams transcended all our shallow hopes
And set a fuse exploding into light.

Our cross lay like a millstone on his heart.
We let him bear the burden all alone.
Now we come forward eloquent with praise,
Our silence broken after he is gone.

Too late! But not too late to change our lot,
To re-evaluate the Negro's gains,
To call together twenty million men
And break the lock that holds us now in chains.

For now we see the fierceness of his truth,
A history of cruelty to our race.
It shall be changed if written with our blood.
His name will be a sign to mark the place.

Oh, Africa! Be gentle to his mound,
For tender is your bosom for your own,
Dark are your nights but filled with stars of hope
That we shall reap the harvest he has sown.

Flight

The dusk comes quietly in
Soon to make way for the night,
The night grows darker and darker,
And is lost in the dawn of light.

Uncertainty

You are two-faced but comrade you are fair.
No one can be certain or foresee,
For those who weep at morn at eve may laugh,
Who live today tomorrow may not be.

You stay on until death steps in,
With fleeting feet you then take flight,
You know death has power over you
As daybreak has power over night.

Then you are gone to plague
Some new-born infant at its mother's breast,
To cling until the final breath is drawn
And that poor soul has lost itself in rest.

As I await the uninvited guest
And you are fading from the darkening room,
I will honor death's command
With growing certainty in my gloom.

I may not see the tears but hear the sobbing
And realize those gathered there are grieving,
But if you stay I'll not know why they weep,
Because I lived or because I'm leaving.

i
The dose of life is fatal in itself.
Beginning indicates there is an end.
The leaves of spring sing many happy songs
But finally are caught in autumn's wind.

At dawn I heralded the newborn day,
At noon I realized it was growing,
When evening came I saw it stooped with age
And as I slept it passed without my knowing.

How often have I watched that night balloon
Shining veiled behind a drifting cloud,
And seen the sun with all its beams of light
Drop suddenly behind an evening shroud.

A rainbow disappearing as you gaze,
A bubble blown and touched and then no more.
Birth and death do not astound this world,
And oceans keep on rolling, dip or pour.

ii
Expect a big return for little spent
While each and everyone feels duty bound?
The Sower really can't expect to reap
From seed that He let fall on stony ground.

iii
Forgotten, now the markers gather moss,
Not one has had a visitor today,
For those who grieved and wept upon the ground
Have dried their tears and gone along their way.

They're balanced, with everything precise —
The millionaire and beggar weigh the same.
The scales were standing still when they went out.
They went as empty-handed as they came.

That same revolving door that whirled them in
Kept turning and has whirled them once again
Into a world of nothingness.
Who knows but that their entry was in vain.

For life is as the lonely blind who reach
And never find the object of the search,
The bird that fills the air with its sweet song
That falls on deaf ears underneath its perch.

Whirl on you tipsy topsy-turvy man,
Keep spinning on, but He who strung the top
Looks down and watches every round you make
And knows when you will wobble, tilt and stop.

It's He who rings the silken curtain down,
No matter how spectacular the show.
Performance done, rewarded? Who can say,
When no one has returned to let us know.

They are worn out and wrecked beyond repair.
The motor stopped that stopped on all the others.
And so the great machine that we call man
Is carted off and junked beside his brothers.

Heaven, ready for reunion
Golden goblets for communion
All the angels now are singing
Music from each harp is ringing
Every scroll is now unrolling
Every bell in Heaven tolling
Sting of death has lost its power
Now has come the greatest hour
Gabriel takes the trumpet.

On the world the dawn is breaking
When there comes an awful quaking
Now the land has started sliding
Sinners look around for hiding
Just as they are bent on fleeing
Dumb are speaking, blind are seeing
As the trumpet's notes are nearing
All the deaf have started hearing
Gabriel, blow the trumpet.

Gabriel, tense with temples pounding,
Gabriel with the trumpet sounding
Mountains now have started skipping
And the moon has started dripping
Sun and stars are now retreating
Trumpet's echoes now repeating
Every wind has started blowing
Every stream increased its flowing
As Gabriel blows the trumpet.

Seas and oceans start their churning
Belching up, their dead returning
Claps of thunder, lightning flashing
Waves against the rocks are dashing
Time has stopped, time is standing
Humble to His great commanding
Clouds are bursting, rain is pounding
All the while the doomsday sounding
Of Gabriel at the trumpet.

Those in Christ are first emerging
Soon the graves will start their purging
Rhyming with the thunder's clapping
Every shroud has started flapping
All the saints begin their shouting
Not a one of them is doubting
Every one of them rejoicing
Everyone His praises voicing
Awakened by the trumpet.

Assembling now the saints are singing
Suddenly like birds when winging
Into Heaven now ascending
Multitudes of them are wending
Some uplifted in a twinkling
By surprise, they had no inkling
Saints are going, going, going
Lifted up by soft winds blowing
Blowing with the trumpet.

Just as all the saints are leaving
Tombs and graves have started heaving
Out the sinners come a-tumbling
Now the thunder's really rumbling
Darkness on the world is creeping
Sinners screaming, sinners weeping
The world is off its axis, reeling
Sinners crying, sinners squealing
Are heard above the trumpet.

Rocks are every exit blocking
Jaws of hell are now unlocking
Earth is crumbling, earth is splitting
And all hell has started spitting
Spitting fumes that start one choking
Sinners now are scorching, smoking
Terror, gripping and appalling
Every sinner, falling, falling
As Gabriel sounds the trumpet.

The hungry mouth of hell is gapping
Flames are licking, flames are lapping
Every wheel in hell is turning
Everything in hell is burning
Everyone in hell is sprawling
Every voice in hell is squalling
To escape is just a notion
For hell is in perpetual motion
Set off by the trumpet.

For Vivian E. Johnson Cook

RIBBONS & LACE

To my sisters
Vera, Doris and Ruth
and to my son
Sterling

Hobo

I'm gonna catch me an armful of freight,
My mamma's dying and I can't be late.
I would buy me a ticket long as I am tall,
Ain't got no money, I'm telling y'all.

Gonna get in a box car, ride them rails,
Gotta see my mamma before she fails.
Won't be no welcome like the prodigal son
'Cause I been a no good son of a gun,
Low down, no good, son of a gun.

Reprobate

She nursed him thru his wheelchair years,
He claimed he was in pain.
She tended him and worked with him
'Till he got on a cane.

He hooked the cane around her neck
To pull her to the bed.
He yanked her face down close to his
And mauled her on the head.

Of course, she died ahead of him
From being dumb and dutiful.
He tossed his cane into her grave
And said, "Bye-bye, you beautiful."

God's Mercy

She was a country teacher
And people called her Miss.
They called her Miss Lillie Bell,
And she was proud of this.

She waved her hands when shouting
And clapped them in the air.
After suffering a stroke,
She said God didn't care.

She said she had found Him out:
"He's as mean as He can be,
How else could He turn his back
On a critter like me?"

She said she had worshiped God,
That she had served Him well.
But since she had a change of heart,
She was on her way to hell.

The devil had his pitchfork
And little imps as well,
Digging 'round to find a place
To put Miss Lillie Bell.

A place was found, Oh yes it was
Right between Heaven and Hell,
A little bit high, a little bit low
And there lies Miss Lillie Bell.

Mr. Body

It was on a Sunday morning
That she shot him dead.
After an all night drinking bout,
She shot him in the head.

The police came and asked her
What time did he die?
"Police, I am telling you,
I ain't got no cause to lie.

"I pulled his gold watch from him
And looked at its face,
It said nine o'clock a.m.
I put it back in place."

Strange, ironic is it not,
He will never drink a toddy.
Like his name, oh what a shame,
He really is a body.

Memphis, 1930

Mr. Shorty is a dwarf and he is black,
He scampers around in a vacant lot,
That's where he makes his moonshine,
The white police think he's a tot.

They think they're seeing a child at play,
Not suspecting him one bit,
He gets good money for his moonshine,
And that's the long and short of it.

Sacrilegious

She said she felt sorry for Jesus
And said he was little and poor.
If she had her way and had her say,
He would never cross her door.

I told her He felt sorry for us,
That's why He was crucified.
She got angry and began to scream,
Claiming that the Bible lied.

She said He was a lil' ole sissy
And had twelve men after Him,
Talking in riddles and parables
And doing it at His whim.

"There's one thing He never counted on,
When He was leading His flock.
Lil' ole sissy, letting men kiss Him,
Well, Judas fixed His clock."

St. Peter

A strange looking man is at my gate,
He looks like a man I know.
The man I know is raggedy,
They call him Ole Bozo.

Ole Bozo was a drunkard,
I thought he would go to hell.
He fussed a lot and cussed a lot
And bootleg he would sell.

This man's been shaved and his hair is cut,
His clothes are all brand new.
Why there's a rose in his lapel
And it's befitting, too.

I guess I'll have to let him in
But then I must be sure.
Maybe Ole Bozo changed his ways,
Maybe his heart is pure.

I can't believe it's Bozo
Here at my gate of bliss.
Come here angels and tell me,
Who in the hell is this?

He hollered, "When you bury me,
Lay my Bible on my chest!
'Cause when I'm preaching down in hell
I wanna do my best."

Now mamma can climb
To the top of the tree
But you're too young

Stand on the ground
Or hold on to the lowest limb
And look up

Ya'll know the reason
I follow Tate around?
'Cause I like to smell his breath,
It's so full of whiskey.

The Letter

There was a crumpled letter on the floor
Of apartment number thirty-four.
The place was quiet and it was bare,
The man had died who once lived there.

The letter read:
"Daddy, I am nine years old today,
Please come home again to stay.
Hurry back, we all miss you,
But don't beat on me like you used to.

"Did you ever stop that drinking, dad?
'Cause when you drink, you sure are bad.
You said you would keep on shooting dice,
Mommy used to say that was not nice.

"Some say you are dead, some say you are not,
I just want to say, I love you a lot.
I guess I'll have to wait and see,
If my letter to you comes back to me.

"Mommy says, about this letter to you,
The mailman always knows what to do.
If you're dead, she says, he won't ring the bell,
He'll write, 'Address unknown, somewhere in hell.'"

Behold

That's the ugliest
Woman I ever saw.
God must have lost
His eyeglasses when
He was making her.

He took my troubles and spanked them,
Told my sorrows to get way back,
Told my tears to stay in my eyes,
Grabbed my sickness and gave it a whack.

When I walk in church on Easter,
I'll be all dressed up in white.
We gonna tear that church up and tear it down,
Yeah, we gonna wreck it with all our might.

I will rock this way and jump that way,
Calling Jesus by his name,
Gonna holler Hallelujah,
That little church will never be the same.

When I walk in church on Easter,
I'm gonna have a lot to say.
I will testify about His goodness
And He'll put my crown in the lay-a-way.

Mystery

Somebody, anybody, please come tell me whether
It's God or the devil that puts couples together

Coma

Not now, not now, please Jesus,
Give her life a little extension.
Lord, please don't take her now,
She just started to draw her pension.

These old feet have carried me around
Back and forth to my stomping ground.
Yeah, these feet have been up late,
Taking me to a red-hot date.

These old feet have walked tiptoe,
When I rolled a guy and stole his dough.
Ain't got no bunions, got no corns
But a devil like me should have horns.

These old feet used to roam and roam,
Always heading away from home.
Oh, they used to dance and they used to prance,
Ooh, La La, even in France.

I'm sorry as hell
That I can hardly walk
But I'm glad as hell
That my feet can't talk.

Flippety flap, flippety flop
We heard the sound some distance away.
We would gather on the porch,
Anxious to hear what he would say.

He always preached about his hand,
Holding it high above his head:
"This old hand still scratches me
And this old hand ain't near 'bout dead.

"This old hand pick white man's cotton,
This old hand make a fist sometime,
This old hand is mad as hell
'Cause the man won't give it a dime.

"I'se walkin' po' soul, tired, Lawd, tired
But keeps on movin' anyhow.
Leavin' wid my hand held high,
I's gittin' on down the road now."

Flippety flap, flippety flop
Flippety flap, flippety flop

Now he is old and feeble
But is known far and wide.
He reads the obituary page
To see whose husband died.

He is a woman chaser,
This man is really one.
He outlived three policies,
Collected and now has none.

I know the rascal personally
And knew his lovely wife.
I think his shenanigans
Were what cut short her life.

He calls himself a ladies' man,
He calls himself a dude.
He's fastidious in his dress
And never is he rude.

He reads the obituary page
To see whose husband died.
His interest in the widow is
Did he leave her well supplied?

He's a con man from his heart,
I give the devil his due.
If your husband dies don't publicize
'Cause he'll be after you.

Some say he lives in Maryland
And some say Tennessee.
I say he lives in Illinois,
Right now, he's after me.

Saturday Night

Took my bath and then jumped sharp,
That was last Sat'dy night.
Shook vanilla flavor on
And was smellin' outta sight.

Got into my Model T
And filled the tank with gas,
Drove that car 'round real slow,
Lookin' for a big brown ass.

Then I seen her all at once
And slyly looked her over:
Big fat tits, big fat but,
I done found four-leaf clover.

Now what we done,
It was not right.
But I'll do it again
Next Sat'dy night.

You're upset because he sleeps with her?
Aw, come on woman, for Heaven's sake,
It's not what he does when he's asleep,
It's what he does when he's wide awake.

Fishermen

"Before I could take off my apron
He dropped two bits into my pocket
Outta the goodness of his heart."
The Lady

He hadn't exactly looked at her,
He always sorta looked down
But she wanted something
Done to her and he did it.

Three red-necked fishermen had
Stumbled upon them.
When they shouted curse words,
She screamed, "Look in my apron pocket!"

She reached in the pocket
And threw the quarter toward them.
One picked it up and the others
Took a fishing line and tied the man.

One fisherman went to the country store,
Took his own money
And bought corn whiskey,
Then asked for a quarter's worth of rope.

He returned to find the woman
Begging that her lover not be harmed.
The bottle was passed and a fisherman
Turned to the woman and said, "You wuz raped, lady."

When she tried to protest,
He shouted, "Goddammit,
White woman,
Didn't you heah?"

Night and Sunshine

At three in the morning,
Woodstock went up one street and down
Another in the black community.
Spotting a lone black man on Wellington,
He pulled over near the curb and waited,
His heart pounding as he heard
The footsteps coming closer.
Nervously, he cleared his throat,
Licked his lips and almost hollered,
"Hey, boy, do you wanna make some money?"

The man walked up to the corner and told him,
"I've got a job at the *Commercial Appeal*
Newspaper and I'm on my way to work.
Go up on Beale Street and you'll find
A Lot of unemployed people."
"Goddamn lazy nigger got a job,
Smart Aleck, too, using a big word, unemployed.
Why didn't he say outta work?
I shoulda run over the black bastard."

Beale Street. Why didn't he think of it before.
He'd been there looking for a black woman,
He would soon be looking for a black man there.
His hands gripped the steering wheel,
His knuckles white.
Driving up a slight hill on Wellington,
He came to Beale and made a right turn.
There were whore houses, a seven-foot-tall
"Long Distances" gambling dive,
Solvent Savings and Fraternal Banks,
The Daisy Theater and Pee Wee's
All-night pool room at which he stopped.

Approaching the 350-pound Pee Wee, the
Visitor remarked, "I want someone to move some
Bootleg whiskey and I'll pay 'em good."
A buxom black whore approached him drinking
Moonshine from a jelly glass.
"Say, white man, white lightening for a white man."
He dared not ignore her and tried to smile
But his thin lips quivered nervously and
He couldn't stop them.
He was saved by a black man named Will Jamison
Who needed money and left with him as he sped away.
Will asked, "Boss, ain't you going pretty fast?"
He answered, "You want some fast money, don't you?"

Arriving at his white clapboard home,
Woodstock pulled into the garage and told
Will to wait there until he called
Him to the back door.
Although it was a wait of a few minutes,
It almost seemed forever and Will wanted
To run, but where?

Finally, the white man called out,
"Nigger, come to the back door."
When Will approached the door,
He was shot, and fell before the white man,
Who screamed:
"A nigger has killed my wife and child!
I shot 'im, I'm holding
His bloody knife! Call the police,
Somebody call the police!"

The police came and three ambulances also.
Will was put in one with a policeman
And a police car accompanied it.
The policeman asked, "Why did you kill
That white woman and child? You're dying
And gotta meet your Maker."
"Boss, I ain't seen no white woman and child.
I knows I'm dying. A red-faced,
Heavysot white man got me
From Pee Wee's place on Beale Street
And promised me some money to move some moonshine.
I knows I'm meeting my Maker."

At Woodstock's house, the police
Discovered the motor of his car was hot
And noticed the night shirt he was
Wearing had the folds of the laundry
In it although he claimed
He was awakened by Will.

When the police returned from
The hospital where Will was pronounced
dead, Woodstock had one question:
"Is the nigger dead? Is the nigger dead?"
When the police answered, "Yes,"
He hollered, "Thang God, thang God,
The niggers dead."

He got "life" for the murder
Of his wife and six-year-old daughter, Arelia.
At his trial, he admitted killing his wife
Because of his love for a white woman called Sunshine.
His voice broke as he spoke of Arelia,
"God, how I loved that child
But she woke up and had to go."

Aint Rachel was an ex-slave,
Mulatto, midwife, and infidel who lived
In Shelby County, Tennessee.
Like a witch riding in on a broom,
She would appear at our house,
Never knocking at the door or announcing herself.
We would happen to look around and there
She was with her little brown dog, Pup,
And her little black bag.

She was a tiny woman with long straight
Mixed gray hair drawn back from her
Forehead which was covered with a damp
Rag filled with gypsum weed to ward off headaches.
Her nose was like a beak and her thin lips curled
Over scattered teeth.
Aint Rachel kept a twig in one corner of her mouth
Which she would now and then dip in her snuff box.
One long tooth protruded.
It was brown from snuff dipping
And it was difficult to tell which was twig
And which was tooth.
Her eyes were like slits and were somber-looking.
Pup seems to have taken on her expression:
He had eyes like slits that had a somber appearance.
Pup was always close to her skirts and
Where they stood or sat they looked
As if they had grown there.
To hear her laugh was frightening:
Her expression at such times never changed.

During winter or summer, Aint Rachel
Wore the same type of clothes,
Several long black skirts and a man's
Suit coat buttoned up and fastened at
The neck with a safety pin.
She would say on a hot day,
"De same thing keep out de cold, keep out de heat."
There was a nutmeg on a string around
Her neck, and tied around her waist was
A blue check apron with a big pocket
In which she carried her snuff box and fresh eggs.

We were small children and would whisper about Aint
Rachel. Mamma would make us go into the next room
And we would push and shove to look thru
The keyhole at her.
We were fascinated by her little black bag
And wondered if there was a baby in it.
Mamma and Papa always used the doctor
To bring babies but it made no difference to Aint Rachel.
Whenever Mamma was pregnant, she came
And sat around, hoping to "ketch de baby."
She'd say to Mamma, "You like
Er settin' hen, can't come out, so I
Come to see you."
We heard other fragments of conversation,
"I jes fed Pup his gun powder and sweet milk.
If anybody bothers me, Pup will *bardaciously*
Et em' up. I can't tarry long,
Gotta go see Martha who swallowed er punkin seed."
She looked at her black bag and said,
"She'll be needin' me soon."

Aint Rachel had another practice, claiming she
Could "fix" any woman so she would get pregnant.
She got quite a bit of money from a white man
Whose wife never conceived.
He was angry and brought his wife back
And was told by Aint Rachel:
"Tell 'er to come inside and I'll zamin' her."
Aint Rachel put the woman on the kitchen
Table and when she finished zaminin' her
Told him, "Aint a thing in de
World wrong wid your wife.
All she need ter
Do is ter change mens."

When mamma asked Aint Rachel to
Come to church sometime,
She answered: "De church is alright till de
Folks git in. Anyway, if its er God
Up there, whuts He hidin' fuh?
Ought to come out in de open.
Yez, de church is full uv washpot
Prayin.' Dat's all 'tis, en He aint hearin' it."
She told how slaves used to turn down
An iron pot, put a stick under it,
Then lie on the ground beside
The pot and pray.
This was done so the pot
Could catch the sound without
Ole Marsa hearing it.
"Hah, de prayers didn't git no further dan de wash pot.
I aint studdin' bout God.
He did't know my mamma en
He don't know me.
My pappy, my slave master, took me from
My mamma at birth and I wuz raised at de big house.
Where wuz God when I was took from my mamma?
Hah, hidin' out!"

Aint Rachel talked about her life
As a child at the big house.
She said that things then were easy,
That she was never sent to the fields to work.
A frequent remark of hers was: "I played
Like er kitten and minded ole missus children."
She added that her father was a doctor
"En made er pet uv me.
Later, my pappy use ter take me
On his rounds ter see de sick.
While he was inside tendin' de sick,
I sat outside and held de hosses.
My pappy used ter give big balls,
And when I grew up I use to dance
Fer de folks, all dressed up
In ribbons en lace.
Got de dresses in my trunk to prove it.
I'll dress up in 'em sometimes — ribbons en lace.

"Yez, my pappy wuz er real doctor.
Why dese newfangled doctors uv today
Will cut yer heart out en call it er tumor.
I'm bettern most uv em, en I
Make es good er medicine es de next one."
When mamma asked her how
She got her medical training,
She was indignant, answering, "Didn't
I set outside en hold de hosses?
Well I'm gwine now, Pup wants ter go."
Even though Pup appeared to be asleep,
With one motion she and Pup got up
And sailed off with Pup practically
Riding the hem of her skirts.

Some days Aint Rachel would talk about white folks,
Which she especially enjoyed doing when
She hadn't been paid for delivering a white baby.
She'd fuss and fume, "I'll 'sick' Pup
On 'em if they ever come 'round me!
Dey lie and de truth aint in 'em.
Claim dey give us freedom, didn't dey?
Dey give it ter us locked in er box
En de white man kept de key.
Try ter bust de box open, like hittin' on dynamite.
Like Pup barkin' et de moon.
Das how far off yer freedom is."

The next day she'd take the Negro for her topic.
Smiling, she'd say, "I'm straddle
De fence and can talk erbout de white en de black.
I'll neer jin Hemp's church,
He's er parson wid concubines.
Undertaker Riggin' will never bury my body;
He's es crooked es er barrel uv snakes.
Now you take Mr. Wilson,
I married him cause he could read."
Each Sunday during Mr. Wilson's
Lifetime, he bathed, dressed
And sat on the front porch and read the paper.
She'd have him sit in the opening
Between the vines so that he could be seen reading.

As we grew older, we were sent to the
Store and had to pass Aint Rachel's house.
Her yard was filled with fig, elderberry,
Mulberry, and peach trees.
There was gypsum weed, sage, mint,
Tansy, and other herbs from which she made medicine.
A bayou swirled and curved through her yard.
There were roosters crowing, hens
Cackling and chicken coops scattered around.

Though the board of health had been after her
To put in a bathroom,
She still had a privy half-hidden by the vines and trees.
She had "sicked" Pup on the man from the board of health
But Pup only wagged his tail.
She excused him by saying,
"I hadn't fed him his gun powder and sweet milk."

Aint Rachel's house was frame and right on the ground,
With two steps leading to the porch.
The windows were covered with shutters and
There was a lattice across the porch covered with vines,
So we could never be sure whether she was
Sitting behind the lattice.
When all at once she would call us,
Afraid, we would hold hands.
Yet we were fascinated by her and would
Sit on the steps as close to her as we could get.
Once she told us she had hoodooed old man Joe Thomas.
She prophesied he would die in a day or so and
Took three sips from a level dipper of
Water and called out "Joe Thomas" three times,
Tossed the water over her left shoulder,
Letting it fall on the ground, then told us,
"I put 'em right back in de ground
Whar he come from."
A few weeks later, when Mr. Thomas died
Aint Rachel took credit for his death.
Not long thereafter, she showed a wisp
Of a woman's hair, put it in an empty
Snuff box and told us, "Someday
If I get mad enough, I'll throw
De snuff box in de bayou. When I do dat,
A certain woman gwine crazy es er bed bug."

Once Aint Rachel asked us, "Wanna see inside my house?"
It sounded sinister but we were lured
Inside a room with half-closed shutters.
There were odd shaped tables, chairs and a high
Bed with a bright colored quilt.
A large picture of Mr. Wilson hung over
The bed and his eyes seemed to follow us.
There were some small plantation pictures
Hanging on the walls.
As we looked at a picture of Negroes
Picking cotton, Aint Rachel said, "My folks."
We saw pictures of white people standing
In front of a big colonial house and
She said, "My folks. But I don't take no stock in 'em."
When we asked to see inside her trunk,
She told us, "Never been opened since Mr. Wilson died."
That scared us and we didn't want to see
Her dresses trimmed in ribbons and lace.

We returned to the porch and asked her
To tell us some tales of slavery.
The one I liked best was about
Her half-brother, Jim.
She said that Jim was a hard working
Man and swore as he chopped cotton
Under the blazing sun.
He would accuse God of "sicking"
The sun on the long rows of cotton.
Aint Rachel related his strange deathbed wish:
He wanted his hoe buried with him.
She smiled and said, "I guess he gwine ter chop his way into
heaben."

On Halloween night, the question was, "Is Aint Rachel out
tonight?"
Just as if she were a lion.
All at once she'd appear, her long skirts
Floating in the air.
She did't need a mask,
All she had to do was come out.
She'd chase us with Pup at our heels barking furiously.
We screamed with fear and delight.

Years passed and somehow I was no
longer afraid of Aint Rachel.
I would sit on her steps as I had as a child.
She could hardly get around because of rheumatism
and great age.
Still, she liked to hear of new babies in the neighborhood.
She'd look at her gnarled hands and remark,
"Dey ketched and spanked er many baby."
Once in a while someone would come for medicine.
She was proud that people remembered her
Medicine and continued to sing her praises as a doctor.
And she continued to let Pup romp
In her backyard until one day he lay
Exhausted at her back door.
Aint Rachel brought him inside and doctored on him
But, despite her medicine, Pup died
A few days later.
I was there when he died and tried
To console her, but her voice was
Filled with sadness as she praised Pup,
"Yez, Pup wuz de best dat ever lived.
He *bardaciously* ate up anybody dat bothered me.
De grave don't mean nothin' ter Pup.
He'll come out if he's er mind ter."
I helped her inside the house and realized that
She was seriously ill.

Mamma and others took food to her but she barely ate.
Though she wore her head rag, she complained of headaches.
Eventually Lena, a niece of hers who came to
Take care of her, asked her if she wanted
Reverend Hemp to come and pray for her.
Mention of his name almost gave Aint Rachel a stroke.
She screamed, "If he come 'round me,
I'll call Pup from de grave!"
She didn't want a doctor and still
Thought her medicine was "es good es de next ones."
However, the doctor came, left some pills
And told Lena that Aint Rachel would not last much longer.

She grew weaker and slept most of the time.
One morning, she just slept away.
When we heard about it, undertaker Riggin
Was carrying her body out.
Aint Rachel's words came back to me:
"He's es crooked es er barrel uv snakes."
The neighborhood was saddened and frightened —
Children hung onto their mothers' skirts.
Suddenly her house had a strange, deserted look
And for the first time we noticed that
Weeds had almost overtaken it.

The day of the funeral came and undertaker
Riggin's place was filled with white and Negro people.
Reverend Hemp walked in, his cane over one arm,
His celluloid collar turned backward.
He wore a frock-tail coat and carried a tattered Bible.
A murmur went through the crowd.
No one seemed to know how it was
That Rev. Hemp was to preach the funeral.
Then there was complete silence.
Reverend Hemp's eyes had a yellowish
Cast and he was feeble from old age.
He placed his feet wide apart to brace himself
And broke the silence by bellowing out:
"Dars great rejoicin' in heaben dis moanin'!
Ah say dars great rejoicin' in heaben dis moanin'!
Ah tell ya, er lost sheep is found!
De angels is singin', Ah tell ya..."
He was off to a good start.
Soon we heard someone coming past
The parlour talking gibberish and laughing
In a high thin voice.
I recalled the words, "If I get
mad enough, I'll throw de snuff
Box in de bayou. When I do dat,
Er certain woman gwine crazy es er bed bug."
My mind was wandering, reviewing the
Many hours spent with Aint Rachel.
From somewhere far off came the
Sound of a dog barking and I recalled
The words: "De grave don't mean
Nothin' to Pup; he'll come out if he's er mind ter."

The choir was singing "Just As I Am"
And Reverend Hemp was wiping perspiration
From his face as I joined the others
To view Aint Rachel.
Some were crying softly and some were scream
"Aint Rachel's gone, gone!"
She looked so tiny, so frail,
So strange.
She was all dressed up in ribbons and lace.

For A. Clifford Brown

Sis Rose

Her husband had a good job
Helping to build the bridge across the
Mississippi River to West Memphis, Arkansas,
But he drank, gambled and chased women.
Coming home on Sunday mornings,
He abused Sis Rose, cursing and striking her.

She told mamma, "I keep praying that one
Of his women will knife him.
He's got a fold on the back of his neck
Deeper than a pork chop eating preacher's.
I keep praying that someone will put
A razor on that fold.
I pray and pray and pray;
I guess God listens but
Don't answer right away.
Seems like God don't want him
And the Devil won't have him,
Trouble enough in Hell.
But God takes his own good time.
I know he hears me because
I prays real loud.
One of these Sunday mornings,
I'll know God heard me
When the white police knock on my door.
When that happens, Sister Johnson,
I'm coming to you with my apron to my face
And I'll be crying tears of joy."

After talking with Mamma,
On leaving, Sis Rose would walk
Through the backyard where we were playing,
Throw up her hand in our direction
And keep on walking, shaking her head.

One Sunday morning, Mamma was
Cooking breakfast and heard a moaning sound.
She opened the back door and
Sis Rose, her apron to her face,
Was coming toward her.

Tenement

She kept half-pints of
Corn whiskey hidden in her flour barrel
And sold them for a quarter
To the others in the Tenement.

Miss Sue and her husband
Were always a little bit tipsy
And on Saturday nights would fight
Until daybreak on Sunday.

She would complain, "John don't blongst
To nothin',
No church, no club,
He just blongst to me."

One Saturday, two big white police
Went to Miss Sue's apartment.
"You Sue White?"
"I'm Sue White but I'm black."

"We can see that.
Where's the corn whiskey?"
"Police, I ain't got none."
Pushing her aside, they searched and found nothing.

When they left, she came out with
A half-pint completely covered with flour.
"Somebody done snitched on me; somebody
Done snitched on me but when God is with you,
The devil can't do you no harm."

That night, she and John started fighting.
His mouth was bleeding and there were bruises
On his face and bald head.
A next door neighbor took him to the county hospital.

Later Miss Sue said, "My snuff don't taste right,
My snuff don't taste right."
She hooked her finger and raked around in her mouth
And out came a piece of John's lip.

She rinsed it off and
Laid it on the mantlepiece.
When the doctors asked if it could be found,
A neighbor took it to them.

Miss Sue said they didn't sew it back on right:
"But one thing, he can't cuss me like he used to.
When he try to call me goddamn bitch,
All he can say is, "You ga da bish!"

Lill

Lill was lying paralyzed
On her left side.
Before I could say a word,
She ordered me to take
A tissue off the top
Of a kleenex box,
To lay aside a pork sandwich
And to take a half-pint of whiskey
From the bottom of the box.

"Take the top off the bottle and hold
The sheet up so the nurse can't
See me drinking."
She drank—glugger, lugger, lugger
Glugger, lugger, lugger—
Until half the whiskey was gone.
I put the bottle back in the kleenex box,
Put the pork sandwich on top of it
And put the tissue back on top.

"How are things on the outside?" Lill asked
"Any man out there got a dollar?"
She raised herself on her good elbow,
Attempted to shake her behind and shoulders
And said, "If a man out there got
A dollar, I git that dollar."

Eventually she walked out of the hospital
As well as anyone:
What led her to walk again
Is a question that boggles my mind.
Was it the pork or whiskey
Or was it the two combined?

A Good Man

You just know he's a good man
And you know he's from the South.
When he spreads a big slow smile,
You see gold teeth in his mouth.

Yeah, you know he's a good man,
When he says "Yes mam, no mam."
Yeah, he's been eating chittlins,
He's been eating smokehouse ham.

He'll call quarters two bits
And he'll call dollars bucks
But you'll really know he's from the South
When you hear him say, "Aw, shucks."

Trick

Bo had no job,
But he had a knife
And hungry kids,
A hungry wife.

Gave her a kiss,
Then he hit the door,
Street all empty,
'Cepting a whore.

"Steel yourself, Bo,
You so uptight,
Gotta a rich white man
For to meet tonight."

Rich old white man
Suspecting no harm,
Led in the dark
To Bo's strong arm.

Robbed and running,
What the white man learn?
That was a trick
That Bo helped turn.

Gossip

Don't blame me for spreading the news,
I thought they had already heard.
I was telling what she told me
And only changed one little word.

Up

Been up all night
And it's jes' 'bout day.
They done sold
My child away.

Took that baby
From my breast.
How they think
I can sleep and rest.

Don't have to get up,
I'm already up.
Lawd knows I'm drinking
From a bitter cup.

Just like the Lord
On the cross.
Where is you, Jesus,
Is you lost?

Tot

"What shall I cook for us today?"
As though she had a choice,
She spoke so softly to herself
With modulated voice.

And as she walked toward the stove
To cook the peas and bread,
She paused to soothe her little tot
And pat its kinky head.

Identical

Come here U.L.
And let me see you.
"Me is not U.L.
Me is V.L."

Naw you aint,
Tell your brother
To come inside
And stand beside you.

Awright, turn your faces thisaway,
Now turn your faces thataway.
Don't move,
Stand still.

One of you is moving,
I don't know which one you is.
Y'all go on
Outside and play.

U.L. you is lagging.
"I is V.L."
Naw you ain't.
"Me is who me say me is, too."

Mamma's Dream

Done sent him off to school
Shined up like a silver dollar—
Shoes polished, britches pressed
And put him on a clean white collar,
Praise God, that boy is gonna be something.

Yes, I see him lead the class,
Hear teacher say, "Your boy don't sass,
He don't even wallow on the grass.
Minnie, your boy is gonna pass."
Told you that the boy gonna be something.

Yeah, I see him finishing school,
I said I'd never raise a fool.
Huh, got a satchel in his hand,
Good Lawd er mighty, he's a lawyer man.
I knowed the boy gonna be something.

Gone straight in the court house, too,
Talking up smart, like lawyers do.
Hear judge say, "You're Minnie's son,
Young man, you have the case done won."

Thank God er mighty, he won the case,
Thank God er mighty, he won the case,
That's my chile, he-is-done-won-the-case
You hear me...

Ole Miss

She was always giving orders:
"Now, Sam, do that, do this."
She hasn't changed since slavery,
She's the same ole southern Miss.

Now Sam knew in the old days
Ole Miss was one big fake.
Tho she tried to be so prissy,
There was chaos in her wake.

Her menfolk sat around her
So gallant and so brave.
It always took a lot of them
To conquer one poor slave.

But Sam is giving orders now
And told her off for good.
She quickly went into her act,
Like a southern Ole Miss should.

She claimed that Sam got "uppety"
And she hollered, "Sam has sassed!"
Her menfolk came er running,
Tho' a hundred years had passed.

Sam says Ole Miss ain't crazy
But kinda cracked instead
And says he's gotta watch her close,
There's a little rock in her head.

"If" Chicago-Style

(In response to Superintendent Willis's challenge
to Negro parents to read Kipling's "If")

If you can turn your head when all about you
    Are empty classrooms waiting to be used,
If you can shift the boundaries to suit you
    And let the black child's learning be abused,
If you can wait and revel in your waiting
    To face up to the segregated schools,
If you can bring in mobile makeshift wagons
    And have the black child work with worn out tools,

If you can dream again of slave and master
    A dream to set us back one hundred years,
If your sweet dream to Negroes is disaster
    Made up of sweat and blood and bitter tears,
If you can overlook your pack of errors
    With conduct unbecoming to the task,
If the various charges lodged against you
    Provide a spotlight, causing you to bask,

If you can talk with parents and ignore them
    Or walk with tots and lose the human touch,
If civil rights groups try and cannot reach you
    And double shifts count, but not too much,
If you can fill black schools to overflowing
    Block education, blast the golden rule,
You'll be a Faubus, Talmadge, or Barnett—
    Or Superintendent of Chicago Schools.

The Surveyor

Oh, I am the greatest surveyor—
Why I'm called to a faraway State.
I use my own rules when I measure for schools,
I can make the line crooked or straight.

They label me racist surveyor,
Standing high on a board makes me free
To see all around little folk on the ground,
In surveillance they look black to me.

I am a wide-ranging surveyor,
I survey, hither, thither, and yon.
My voice is like thunder, is it any wonder
You can see the board shake that I'm on.

Some call me the unfair surveyor,
Well, I am best when looking at me,
I look myself over and pronounce "Four-Leaf Clover"
From the board comes "Eureka, Oh Gee!"

I just know I'm the greatest surveyor,
I am paid so much more than I'm due,
I whirl in and out, I resign and I pout
And I take the back door when they sue.

Yes, I am the sentry surveyor,
I can see from the top of my wall
Willis wagons around the southside of town
And a warehouse befitting a stall.

My hide is as thick as old Jumbo's
And no one has pricked the first layer,
I don't even wince for it makes all the sense
That I should be my own surveyor.

Oh, I am the stunt man surveyor,
I see well when I cover my eyes,
If they held an exam, I would top Alabam
And Wallace would hand me the prize.

Conventioneering

You people really messed things up
And tricked Ole Marsa, too,
By staying home, watching TV
And getting me in this stew.

That Shoot to Kill meant blackbirds,
That Maim and Cripple, too,
That is the law and order
I had reserved for you.

The mace I had for your black face,
The fences and defenses
Were used against these people,
Rattling all my senses.

Now let me just explain one thing,
My paper was really white,
You people call it hogwash
But hogs need washing, right?

You people made all hell break loose,
And now want pigs in pens.
It is my contention, you fouled the convention
And I say that with two sets of chins.

"When up at Pick Pack at the Shoppin' Center,
Two big red-faced white police taken me
And put me in a squad car.
I knows a little bit 'bout the Bible
And was sayin' to myself and sorta hummin' real low,
'I is weak, thou is strong; I is weak, thou is strong.'
All at once I seen Mr. Oliver looking for me,
I clambed over them white police and jumped out,
Hollerin', 'Free at last, free at last,
Thank God amighty, I'm free at last!'

"After that time you hear King's at one place,
Then he at another place makin' folks mad.
He stirred up so much trouble I knowed sumpin' had to give.
I said to myself, 'Why don't he do like I do,
I goes in my house and shet my door.'
Police is all over the place wid tear gas,
Can't go to the laundry and wash clothes.
Everthing is closed down since he came in here the last time.
He didn't go in his house and shet he door,
That's how come he was shot.
I don't feel sorry for him,
I feel sorry for myself 'cause
I can't go to Pick Pack and buy me no mo' whiskey."

Defense

De fence they keep on talking 'bout
Must gonna be powerful strong.
Done taken all them soldier boys,
Must gonna be powerful long.

Done ask us all to help with it
And I can't figger why
Unless that it's gonna be
A fence that's mighty high.

De forest we been savin'
Will be split up for de rails.
We got to make it strong they say
And hammer it with nails.

They say de enemy is awful,
Say he likely to commence
For to messin' with the country
If he break in through de fence.

If he ever charge at me
Just like he ain't got no sense,
I ain't gonna stand there like er fool,
One of us gonna jump de fence.

I Got Since

I sho is glad what they done
In all the ghetto schools,
Taken the teachers' straps away
But that don't make us fools.

They know they cannot whip us,
They cannot push or shove.
My mamma say, "You go to school
Potected by my love."

They claim I cannot reed or rite,
I rit on all the halls,
Had since to break the windows,
Mark on the outside walls.

And I go on ter college, too
Wid my big bushy head.
All my since is in my hair,
My brain? It done been dead.

Out

Some people stay and fret it out
Some people stay and sweat it out
Some stay and try to buck it out
And timid ones just duck out

Some grab their things and haul out
And scary ones just crawl out
Some can smoothly move out
While others have to prove out

Some stay and try to hold out
While others have been sold out
Some gab until they talk out
Others pick up and walk out

There's one thing
I'm going to spell out
Whitney, you had the grit
To get the hell out

Johnnie Thomas

You will be missed by Labor Dispute,
You're leaving the job with good repute.
The friends you have made all wish you well
And they will be phoning or ringing your bell.

Modest, reserved and capable, too,
Is just part of the tribute that we pay you.
Faithful, loyal, Johnnie-on-the-Spot
But now you will have a different lot.

You'll get up refreshed from sleeping late
And I predict you will find your mate.
But don't you take up with some loud shuffler
Whose brakes don't work and who's lost his muffler.

Generator gone and ignition, too —
Well, Johnnie, he's not the one for you.
His battery should be good, automatic transmission —
Johnnie, you're in for a helluva transition.

166

Country Singing

I don't mean to boast or brag,
Folks, I've got a magic touch,
What I want, I always get
And it's a little too much.

I poured my buddy some moonshine
That he said was just like scotch,
Then he clinked his glass against mine
And said, "Here's to you, you're top notch."
I'm a humdinger

I saw a girl that caught my eye.
She said, "Pleased to meet you, country boy,
I hope you like staying 'round here."
She had on gloves and was acting coy.

The guys all said, "You can't get that girl.
She's highfalutin' and bigity,"
But when I kissed her and held her close
Her heart was er pounding, Hot zigity!
I'm a humdinger

That's not all I got to say.
Come on you girls and try me out,
I betcha when I start to bill and coo
You'll start screaming and jump up and shout.

Can't help it, doggone it, dad gummit,
I'm a humdinger, humdinger

Harry's Lamb

Harry had a little lamb
That didn't have a voice,
But everytime she opened up
Proud papa did rejoice.

He followed her career up close,
Kept her beneath his wing,
And it made papa laugh and shout
To hear his baby sing.

And so a critic turned out
Her singing to appraise.
When Harry read the critic's view,
He really was amazed.

With flashing eyes and balled up fist
And cuss words ready, too,
Old Harry hollered out the words,
"I'm er coming after you.

"My baby sings, I say she sings,
I heard her hit high C.
If you don't like the way I talk,
Come on and challenge me.

"My baby sings, and that is that,
Don't mess with Uncle Sam.
I'll land a punch right in your nose,
You talked about my lamb.

"Now tell the others that I say
When I come off this stool,
I'll run around and punch 'em good
And show folks I'm no fool."

The Comeback

I see 'em point the finger
As I go strolling by
And I hear 'em whisper "Has been"
But that don't make me cry.

But I do sigh
When I think of the old days, the show days,
When heydays were heydays
And paydays were paydays.

I was a great dancer then,
My name glistened on Broadway
Like a cop's badge
On a dark night.

I was billed as Zanobia
The dancer from India,
But now like everybody else
I'm billed once a month.

I remember my manager saying one day,
"Zanobia, you need a make up"
And I said, "I ain't
Makin' up to nobody."

"But Zanobia, you're
A great dancer,
You need
A build up."

So at the fluffy-ruffle counter at Sears
I said, "Girlie, I need a build up."
She asked, "One like Dagmar's, one with a plunge?"
I said, "Yes, dearie, make it sponge."

That night the lights were sparkling,
The band was playing
And I was dancing,
Slightly swaying.

The applause was tremendous,
At the curtain call
And, smiling, I was
Hoping nothing would fall.

Bowing low, just like Dagmar,
Until the very end,
When suddenly I lost
My bosom friend.

But I really was good,
Please believe me,
Why they told me so,
They wouldn't deceive me.

I was a
Lena Horne,
I horned in
Wherever I could.

I was a Katherine Dunham,
A la Josephine Baker,
I was a Gilda Gray,
The Shimmie Shaker.

My public would say,
"There she goes
With the million dollar legs."
Now they call them old broken down pegs.

They now say, "Slow down, Zanobia,
That's too much for your age."
Oh, but my best performance
Was not done on a stage.

Oh, they call me Old Sack,
They call me Old Hag.
I'll show 'em what's left
In this old bag.

I'll make a comeback
For the show must go on.
Give me some hot music
And I'll shake every bone.

Tubes in the nose, needles in the veins,
Strange machines around the bed.
The EKG is standing still,
Got no pulse, hell, the patient is dead.

Aw, come on all you Docs out there,
Come on off that brain wave jive.
Heart stopped beating, but not yet dead,
Well, my grandma was buried alive.

Palo Alto

So the rooster woke you up too soon
With all of his loud crowing.
He was feeling awfully proud,
That rascal was really glowing.

The chicken coop belongs to him,
He rules that roost alone.
With six nests all with eggs,
He's a king on his throne.

So don't complain about the guy,
It's a wonder he didn't shout.
With six hens all to himself,
He has something to crow about.

Wino

That wino guy with his complaint,
I should have said his gripe.
Oh boy, was he a nuisance
So full of bunk and tripe.

He and some Polish motorman
Were mixed up in a fight,
He claimed that he was kicked —
I think it served him right.

He talked to everyone around,
Just talking, yap, yap, yap,
He said the guy knocked out some teeth
And showed a great big gap.

He ridiculed the Poles,
The Irish and the Jews
But it was on the Poles
He heaped the most abuse.

Announcing he was Swedish,
He pounded on his chest.
Oh, they were honest people,
The finest and the best.

He pounced again on "races"
and would have got to mine
But I gave him a dirty look
Which he took as a sign.

He punctuated every phrase
With sons of so and so's
And yet he wanted sympathy
When telling of his woes.

He said he'd wined for breakfast,
He ranted and he swore.
Why I'm surprised that it's his back
He claims is very sore.

Here's to you, transit motorman,
You know riff-raff from class.
Buy why did you kick him in his back
Instead of in his ass?

Black Garbage Man

He asked if he could
use the word nigger
in my presence and I
said of course you may.

"These niggers over here
are high-toned,
They throw garbage in the
alley and we have to clean it up."

I asked if they didn't know
they were being helped by him
and he said, "No, mam, they treat
us like dirt under their feet."

I autographed a book of mine
and gave it to him.
His wife asked, "Where did you get
something like this from"? and was told

"From the lady who lives among
those high-toned niggers.
She gave it to me and told me I'd
be reading poetry, which they don't read."

Sunrise

Yesterday was pregnant with today,
Last night grew weary and forlorn,
Then old midwife dawn came creeping in
And the world is mother to the morn.

Slate

The world is but slate and we the chalk.
What would we give to see the slate effaced
To try to make a better mark?
But none has marked again when once erased.

Fate

Be wise and go along without complaint
For fate will not be bucked nor be subdued.
The woodman spared the tall and sturdy oak,
Then along came the wind and it was hewed.

Let no one tell you where, when or why
But ponder what I say for what it's worth.
The coin was tossed, the mighty die was cast,
Your fate already sealed before your birth.

Humanity

If I am blind and need someone
To keep me safe from harm,
It matters not the race to me
Of the one who takes my arm.

If I am saved from drowning
As I grasp and grope,
I will not stop to see the face
Of the one who throws the rope.

Or if out on some battlefield
I'm falling faint and weak,
The one who gently lifts me up
May any language speak.

We sip the water clear and cool,
No matter the hand that gives it.
A life that's lived worthwhile and fine,
What matters the one who lives it?

For Avery Krashen

Life

This is life said the sailor boy
As he sailed the restless sea.
Oh, give me the waves and the billows,
It's a sailor's life for me.

But this is life said the mother
As she held her firstborn close.
This is the life I've longed for,
The life I love the most.

But this is life said the farmer boy
As he walked behind the plow.
Just then the evening breeze came 'long
And kissed him on the brow.

What is life to me is not life to you,
It's the joy we get from the things we do,
And that joy in spite of strife
Keeps the world turning, and so that's life.

The Holy Man

I met a man who had a holy look
And in his hand he held the holy book,
When questioned as to when and why
Was just as mystified as you and I.

Once more he opened the holy book
And with his finger traced the words he read,
And never found a scripture that could prove
That we shall live again after we're dead.

Recall that here's a man who preaches resurrection
Of meeting with the Father and the Son,
Of Life beyond the grave that is perfection,
Oh, mercy, mercy, on this frightened one.

Me sit upon the right-hand side of Him,
The candle snuffed out that once He lit.
Just what would He and I converse about
With Him almighty wise and me no wit?

The artist laid down his brush,
The poet laid down his pen,
They gazed at a glorious sunset
That defied the genius of men.

The leaves on the trees glistened
With drops of the recent rain.
Somewhere a bird sang out a note,
A mixture of joy and pain.

The stillness was as lovely
As the colors in the sky.
There was reverence for the sunset
That was quickly slipping by.

The poet turned to the artist and said,
"Brush what you have painted away
And write on your canvas these words instead,
'The magnificent death of a day.'"

For Thomas N. Todd

Wings

Yesterday's fire is but ashes,
Yesterday's snowman is gone.
Last summer's rose is pressed and dry,
Who knows where the robin has flown?

The bell in the tower rings midnight,
No echo is left of its tone.
A shooting star goes across the sky
And no one knows where it's gone.

The Reaper is out for the harvest.
Farewell, farewell is the cry.
So close behind the gay hello
Comes the sad but sure goodbye.

The hillside has washed to the valley
Whose waters were drained by the sea,
The sea's ship has sunk in disaster,
Oh, where can its occupants be?

For David Roediger

The sky the tent for one continuous scene,
Each one is forced to play and play alone.
Birth gives the cue to get on stage,
Its only task is calling out, "You're on."

There is no synopsis of the play
Where comedy and tragedy are spun,
Suspense and drama tightly woven in,
No actor knows how long the show will run.

Just one makes up the audience and He
Controls and motivates the entire horde,
The brainchild of His weird, fantastic dream
And He manipulates the velvet cord.

Each leaves as the curtain is drawn,
Some thinking it is written in the script
That they will rest forever at the end,
Sleeping soundly in the crypt.

Thus some have lain for centuries, they say,
And others have another tale to tell,
That some who blundered joined another show,
A tragic scene, the platform set in hell.

Mother Earth

You give the trees a place to plant their roots,
In you the tiny flower makes its bed,
Volcanos leap at but a nod from you
And earthquakes hit if you but shake your head.

Your palm outstretched holds food for all who till,
Your secret pockets are filled with jewels rare,
Geologists keep probing in your veins
To find the treasures you have hidden there.

A child of yours yet prodigal am I,
It is so strange that you and I are one,
So unalike and yet so very close,
The Potter must be sad for what He's done.

Someday I will come back to you to rest,
Returning as the hunted to its cave.
Oh, earth, do not deny your own
But welcome me with fresh and open grave.

For Jack Bulmash

Temptation

I was offered roses,
There were thorns,
I did not reach.
I was offered jewels:
lustrous pearls, dazzling rubies
and beautiful sapphires,
I was not impressed,
Again, I did not reach.

I was offered longevity,
I did not reach
for old age and its problems.
Alas, I was offered peace,
quiet and rest.
With all my heart and soul
I reached — and
embraced death.

Elma Stuckey is the granddaughter of former slaves. Born in Memphis in 1907, she came to Chicago with her husband and two children in 1945. She has worked as hat check girl, maid, rural school teacher, head nursery school teacher, and supervisor for the Illinois Department of Labor. Her poems have been enthusiastically received by white and black, at such colleges and universities as Harvard, Cornell, Wisconsin, and Malcolm X, as well as at high schools and community organizations. She is the mother of Sterling Stuckey, the distinguished historian and author at Northwestern University.